WHAT CAN I SEE in the POLAR REGIONS?

Annabel Griffin
illustrated by Rose Maclachlan

HUNGRY TOMATO™

First published in Great Britain in 2021
by Hungry Tomato Ltd
F1, Old Bakery Studios,
Blewetts Wharf, Malpas Road
Truro, Cornwall, TR1 1QH, UK

A CIP catalog record for this book is available from the British Library.

ISBN 978-1-913440-17-6

Manufactured in the USA

Discover more at
www.hungrytomato.com

CONTENTS

Words in bold capital letters **LIKE THIS** can be found in the glossary.

WHAT CAN I SEE IN THE POLAR REGIONS?

The polar regions are the coldest places on Earth! Can you spot the animals that make these freezing lands their home?

THE ANTARCTIC

COOL PENGUINS

Lots of different types of penguin can be found in the Antarctic. They are birds but they can't fly. Their wings act more like flippers.

Wobbly walkers

On land, penguins get around by waddling, jumping and sliding on their bellies.

Flying in water

Penguins are excellent swimmers and spend over half of their time in the water, where they hunt for food.

Proud parents

Mom and dad share parenting duties.

Babysitting

Male emperor penguins look after eggs until they hatch.

Love birds

Penguins are very sociable animals. They live in large groups and form couples to breed and raise chicks.

That can't be comfortable!

Some penguins build nests out of rocks.

UNDER THE ICE

These sea animals all have BLUBBER, a thick layer of fat under their skin, which helps to keep them warm in the freezing water.

Color changing whales

Beluga whales are born grey or brown and only turn white when they become adults.

Curious creatures

Minke whales are very nosey. They will often approach boats in the water to see what's going on.

Unicorns of the sea

The narwhal's famous "horn" is actually an overgrown tooth. No one knows for certain what it's for.

Team players

Killer whales work together in groups called *pods* to gang up on their **PREY**, including penguins and seals.

BRILLIANT BEARS

Polar bears are specially ADAPTED to living in the Arctic, but it isn't always easy for them. They spend most of their time searching for food, which can be very hard to find.

See-through fur

Their fur may look white, but it's actually **TRANSPARENT!** Light bounces off it, making the bear look white, and helping them to blend in with the snow.

A playful pair

Polar bear mom's usually give birth to twins. Cubs will stay with their mother for just over two years.

Splashing about

Polar bears are good swimmers. They use their giant front paws like paddles.

What's for dinner?

Polar bears are **CARNIVORES**, which means they mostly eat meat. They're favorite meal is seal!

JOIN THE PACK

Arctic wolves live in groups called *packs*. There are normally 5-8 wolves in a pack, and they work together as a team when they go hunting.

A varied diet

Arctic wolves are carnivores. They mostly hunt musk oxen and caribou (reindeer) but will also eat seals and other smaller animals and birds.

Sensational senses

Wolves have great eyesight, hearing, and sense of smell, to help them track down food.

Follow the leader

The leader of the pack is known as the *Alpha*. He is the strongest male in the group.

Wrapped up warm

They have two thick layers of fur to help keep warm. The outer layer is completely waterproof.

FROZEN FLIPPERS

These flippered friends all belong to a family of animals called *pinnipeds*, which includes seals, sea lions and walruses.

Elephant Seal

Big seal, big nose

Elephant seals are the largest type of seal. Males have strange, trunk-like snouts.

Long in the tooth

A walrus's tusks continue to grow throughout its life. A male's can reach just over 3 feet in length.

Walrus

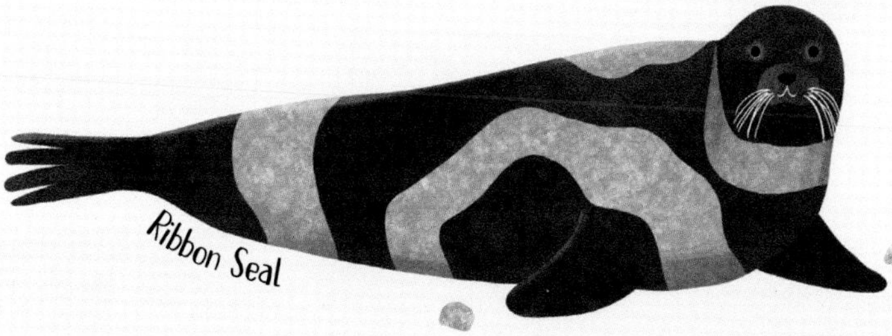

Flipper footed

Instead of feet, seals have two back flippers. These are great for swimming, but not for walking!

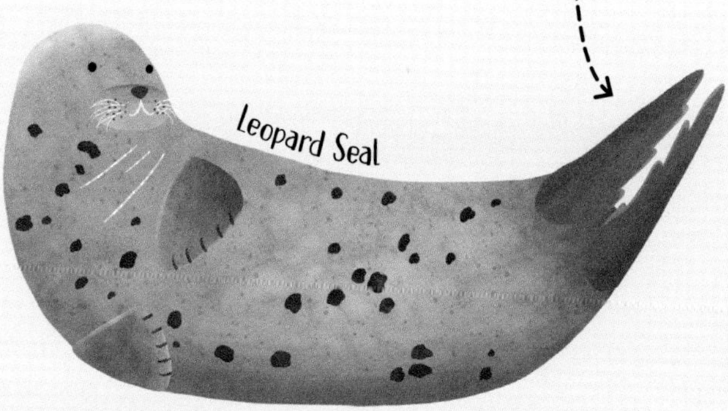

Hide-and-go-seek

This pup's fluffy white fur is perfect **CAMOUFLAGE** against the snow. It will help to keep it hidden from **PREDATORS** until it learns to swim.

Deep breath!

Seals can hold their breath underwater for up to two hours!

FEATHERED FRIENDS

Some birds, like the snowy owl, don't mind the cold, but others will fly away to warmer places for the winter. This is called MIGRATION.

Changing feathers

Ptarmigan's **MOLT** twice a year. Their feathers are white in the winter and brown in the summer.

Sensing in the snow

Snowy owls have excellent eyesight and hearing to help them find their prey in the snow.

From pole to pole

Every year, the Arctic tern travels all the way from the Arctic to the Antarctic Circle and back again - the longest migration in the world!

Stop thief!

The sneaky Arctic skua will often steal food from other birds in mid-air.

Deep divers

Not only can puffins fly, they can also swim! They will dive up to 200 feet in search of fish to eat.

LIFE IN THE TUNDRA

Tundras are large open areas of frozen land where hardly anything grows. These animals have special features to help them survive there.

Woolly beasts

Musk oxen have very long, shaggy woolen coats to help them keep warm in the freezing winters.

Snow hoppers

Arctic Hares have long back feet and strong legs to help them move quickly in the snow.

Dashing through the snow

Caribou have large, two-toed hooves, which help them travel easily across snow and are useful for digging through ice to find food.

Fluffy feet

Arctic foxes have fur on the bottom of their feet to protect them from the cold snow and ice.

WHERE IN THE WORLD?

The polar regions are found at the very top and bottom of the Earth. Here is a circular map of each region, showing which animals live where.

ARCTIC CIRCLE
(Northern Polar Region)

South Pole
ANTARCTICA
Southern Ocean
ANTARCTIC CIRCLE
(Southern Polar Region)

DID YOU KNOW?

Tough Tusks

Walruses use their tusks to drag themselves out of the water. They must be super strong!

A whopping weight!

Male elephant seals weigh up to 4.4 tons. That's more than the weight of 5 large polar bears!

What's in a name?

Killer whales aren't really whales, they're dolphins. They are pretty good killers though!

WHO WAS HIDING?

Did you spot the little lemmings playing hide-and-go-seek in each polar scene?

Lemmings are small rodents that can be found in the Arctic. They measure between 5-7 inches.

During the winter, lemmings live in tunnels under the snow, to keep warm and to hide from their many predators.

Lemmings are a favorite snack of the snowy owl but are also eaten by many other animals including Artic foxes, Arctic wolves and polar bears.

GLOSSARY

adapted (adaptation) - when a living thing has become able to survive in its surroundings by developing special features/skills over a long period of time.

blubber - a special layer of fat under the skin that is used for warmth.

camouflage - to look like something else so as not to be easily seen.

carnivores - animals that mainly eat meat.

migration - traveling from one place to another at different times of year.

molt - to lose feathers, skin or hair. Many animals molt in the summer as a way to keep cool. Sometimes this makes them change color.

predators - animals that hunt and kill other animals for food.

prey - an animal that is hunted by other animals for food.

sociable - sociable animals/people are friendly and like spending time with others.

transparent - clear or see-through, like glass.

The Author

Annabel Griffin is a writer and artist based in the Southwest of England. She is passionate about nature and loves hiking and gardening. *What Can I See...?* is her first series of books for children.

The Illustrator

Rose Maclachlan is an illustrator based in Devon, who recently graduated from Falmouth University with a BA in Illustration. She likes to experiment with collage and texture to create her work and takes inspiration from her love of the outdoors and the beach.